"I am reading Proust for the first time. Very poor stuff. I think he was mentally defective."

- Evelyn Waugh

スタジオウェナ

Published in the United States of America.

A スタジオウエナ Production
Austin, Texas, USA
ISBN-13: 978-1537323824
ISBN-10: 1537323822

On Making Madeleines

With Pictures & Recipe

WENA POON

スタジオウェナ

マドレーヌ手引き書

瑪德琳蛋糕秘籍　方慧娜

On Making Madeleines

OR, HOW TO SPEND A LOT OF TIME PERFECTING SOMETHING WHICH YOU CAN JUST AS EASILY BUY FROM A STORE

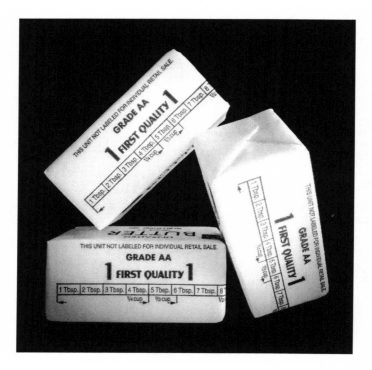

D'abord,
Wear your best linen apron

THE THING ABOUT baking French things like madeleines is that you can't rush them.

They were made by people with a lot of time: 19th century bakers, nuns, indulgent mothers for invalids. You really should just buy them from a good store whenever you want to eat them. If you've taken the trouble to buy this little book, it's probably because someone gave you a madeleine pan. Or, like me, you finally bought one after twenty years of evaluating the pros and cons of owning yet another glamorous kitchen tool that would see little use.

So if you have the damned pan, either hang it on the wall as a sculptural ornament, or use it at least once. I wrote this to help you use it at least once, and successfully. I will tell you all the stuff that Internet recipes and cookbook authors never bother to tell you.

As the Japanese – perfectionists – like to say, *mazu*...(first...) Or, if you really want to be French, *d'abord*...*D'abord,* wear your best linen apron. You know, the kind that everybody in *Monocle* magazine wears. You have to get into the role. It is Cosplay Time. Role: Polished Peasant.

Ensuite, sprinkle purifying salt all over your kitchen to prepare yourself for this holy ritual. Women readers – you are not allowed to attempt this if it's *that* time of the month, because you are Dirty. 冗談だよ！ *I'm joking.*

Make sure you have 3 continuous hours to spend at home if you want to bake them from start to finish. Helps if you're watching a movie on the telly, like *Chocolat* with Juliet Binoche, which is inspirational, or *A Walk In The Clouds* with Keanu Reeves, which is a very dumb eye candy movie set in a Mexico vineyard that is perfect for not really paying attention to. Don't watch *Babette's Feast*: she makes too many complicated dishes. You'd just feel nervous.

East Asian women readers need not be confined to Western films. As television programmers in Asia remind us every festive season, it is our prerogative to watch martial arts films to celebrate our bloodthirsty heritage. Baking is such a dull activity that you should have things like *Hakuoki: Demon of the Fleeting Blossom*, or *Samurai X: Trust & Betrayal* running in the background. These swashbuckling films are very boring except for the fighting parts. Because the duelists would spend some time announcing their name and background, before unleashing the first testosterone-charged battle cry *aaaaaarrrrr!*, you have plenty of time to stroll out of the kitchen, hands in your linen apron pockets, to catch a handsome jawline, the swing of a samurai ponytail, and the awesome sight of blood splattering on rice paper screens. The moment the film reverts back to the big-eyed girl crying over her fallen man amid tumbling cherry blossom petals, go back to the kitchen.

Once you have chosen your background entertainment, make sure your kitchen counter is clear of stuff because you'll need to spread out. Also, check that you have space in your fridge (who does?) to fit a mixing bowl and later the madeleine tray itself for the chilling steps.

Be in a good, patient mood when you undertake this. Because it's such a pain, it might be worth investing in two madeleine trays so you can bake a big bunch each time. However, they take up space in your kitchen cupboard. Worse, they may bake unevenly since both trays may not fit in the middle rack of the oven. Consider the seriousness of uneven baking. I'm sure you never have. Since not all of them will be in the sweet spot in the center of your oven, your madeleines will come out *some browner than the others*. They will not have a uniform yellow color. If they don't have a uniform yellow color, then they won't look exactly like something that issued forth from the hands of Julia Child, or from the refrigerated display at Starbucks, which is the whole point you are attempting this shallow enterprise.

Therefore, it may not be sensible to acquire two madeleine trays. Just as it was never sensible to acquire that second kitten.

"Toby needs a friend..." my husband had argued.

"Toby has a friend. You. Me."

"He needs a cat friend. If you have one cat, you might as well get two so they can keep each other company. It's not twice the work, really, it's economies of scale."

Lies. All lies. It's twice the poop, twice the cat hair.

Should you buy one or two madeleine trays? I don't know. Basically, with madeleines, you're damned if you do and you're damned if you don't. More on that later.

I have tried many recipes by eminent cookbook authors. Some worked; many just crashed and burned. Did these authors actually do it or they were just bluffing? I could feel their disregard and negligence, their utter *mépris* for fellow human beings. It seeps through their 'foolproof' recipes.

The madeleine tray I use is the 16-mold Goldtouch tray from Williams-Sonoma, but any madeleine tray you would suffice, as long as you're prepared to try again if your first batch wasn't what you expected. The amount of batter in my recipe fills 16 molds, so if you have an 8-12 mold tray, you may have extra batter, which you can chill and keep for a few days to try again.

Did you hear correctly? Madeleine trays have *different* numbers of molds? Yes. My recipe is sized for 16 molds per tray. That makes 16 madeleines. Some trays make only 12, some 18. If you use a recipe for a 16 mold tray and, halfway through the laborious process, you realize that you miscounted and your tray does *not* have 16 molds, you're fucked. But if you were that good at arithmetic, why would you even be interested in reading a book about a cookie made famous by a French novelist? I've outted you, English majors. You wouldn't even care about this cookie if it weren't for that man. Well, the very first page of this book tells you what I think of his work. Sock it to him, Evelyn!

Be careful now, English majors. I'm going to have to start talking about numbers, even fractions. Helmets, on!

Step 1: Dry Ingredients Mixing (5 min)

Shoo all pets away.

Get ready 1 small mixing bowl and these things:

- 2/3 cup all-purpose flour

- 1 teaspoon baking powder

- Tiny, tiny pinch of salt (but definitely omit if using salted butter, otherwise madeleine will be too salty. I say "tiny, tiny" because the salt isn't for flavor, it's to bring out other flavors. If you have a heavy hand with salt, trust me, salty madeleines are not very good to eat at all)

Sift this stuff together into mixing bowl and then set it aside. See? It wasn't that hard.

This easy step is designed to give you a false sense of security.

Continue to shoo pets out of the kitchen. Eat some jelly beans for energy for next step.

Step 2: Wet Ingredients Mixing, then Chill Time (1 hour 10 minutes)

Get ready a larger mixing bowl. This bowl has to be larger than the bowl in Step 1. *C'est très important*, because the dry ingredients would also eventually go into this larger bowl, and if you reversed the order, you will be very sorry, because you cannot put big things into small ones. I've tried.

If you actually only ever own 1 mixing bowl, at this point you either have to go find some other receptacle, or drive to the store to buy more mixing bowls. If you are driving to the store anyway, why don't you go pickup some store-bought madeleines and forget the whole thing? Costco sells them by the pail for a reasonable price.

You are still here?

Get ready your handheld electric whisk, and these things:

- ½ cup butter (unsalted)(if using salted butter, omit the pinch of salt in Step 1).

- 2 large eggs

- 1/3 cup sugar

- 2 tablespoons milk (bring to room temperature)

- 1 tablespoon honey - I really don't know why this is needed since we're already using sugar, and you can't taste it in the final product anyway, but at this point I'm too superstitious to leave it out

- Nice to have: Grated zest of 1 lemon (or orange) — if you don't like your madeleines too lemony or orangey, and prefer a more neutral flavor, use half a lemon instead of a whole one, or just omit this entirely, why bother

- 1 teaspoon best quality vanilla extract - I've used seeds from a real vanilla bean from the 'famous' Nielsen-Massey, instead of vanilla extract, and it made absolutely no difference in the final outcome, so save yourself the expense and just use extract

First, soften the butter. Because it's likely you don't have any softened butter just sitting around, like cookbook authors expect you to have. Put the butter in a small bowl and microwave for 10 seconds. Take it out, break it down with a knife, then microwave for another 10 seconds. It should be soft without turning into oil. If your butter has turned to hot oil because you have overheated it in an attempt to soften it, and you are lazy and use it anyway to make the batter, it would make a rocky madeleine that looks deep fried. Don't say I didn't tell you.

Put sugar in bowl. Using pastry cutter or fingertips, rub sugar and zest (or vanilla seeds) together until they're moist and fragrant. I have to thank cookbook author and chef Dorie Greenspan for inventing this step: I've never seen it in other recipes and I really like it because it smells nice.

Add the 2 eggs. Using handheld electric whisk, whisk for 2 minutes until mixture thickens slightly. Don't try to make the mixture puffy by whisking for even longer; there is no point.

Add the honey and vanilla. Whisk a bit more.

Gently fold in the flour in 3 separate batches with a spatula. DON'T RUSH IT. Don't overmix and push all the air out of the eggs. You want the madeleines to be fluffy. Julia Child said once that it is preferable to have unmixed bits, than to overmix and deflate the batter. Julia Child lies. If you have unmixed bits, they will bake and taste exactly that – unmixed. You just have to learn how to fold and mix evenly without letting all the air out. If you don't know how, ~~it takes practice, don't worry~~ *God help you.*

Now fold in the melted butter and stir gently. Try to get all the butter smoothly incorporated so there are no little butter knobs floating around.

Then stir in the room temperature milk. If you add cold milk to this batter, it would cause the melted butter to harden, so your batter would begin to look granular with tiny lumps of butter. So make sure the milk isn't straight out of the fridge. I've baked the granular batter and it turned out ok, but still, why take the chance. The road is strewn with thorns ahead.

The batter should now be smooth and shiny. (Sometimes it isn't – I have no idea why. Barometric pressure?) Put plastic wrap on the top to keep it from drying out and put in fridge for 1 hour or up to 2 days. That's why I warned you that you need 3 continuous hours for this project. 冗談じゃねいぞ！*No joke.* I've tried a recipe where there was no chilling step — it said to mix the batter then go into the oven directly. I ended up making oily rock cakes.

Chilling the batter lets the flavors meld and makes it easier to handle when filling the mold. The main reason, however, has to do with achieving the characteristic "bump" through the "thermal shock" that people talk about. Which I shall cover in the next chapter, because I intend to go on about it.

Ensuite,
The Madeleine Bump and other Oddities

WHILE YOUR BATTER is chilling, let's digress. Otherwise I'll never have enough pages to print this into a proper book, and I'd have to end up publishing all this in a form which I disdain: the 'BLOG'. Why do they call it a 'blog'? I've forgotten. Is it a contraction of 'Web log'? But why was it called 'Web log' in the first place? And how did *that* come to replace a book? Fuck those guys.

I was talking about the thermal shock and the bump on madeleines. Some madeleines have such ugly and tall protrusions that they look like pregnant guppies. I prefer mine to have just the slightest swell and a little broken, but if the bump doesn't happen I don't really care. There are amateur bakers out there that threaten to commit ritual suicide if their madeleines don't bump. I am serious. They tend to write those 'BLOG' things. I have no pity for them.

For me, the most important thing is to achieve a madeleine that is yellow, fluffy and rich, and not oily, overly salty or perfumey.

Madeleines are traditionally flavored with orange blossom water. That used to sound so nice and exotic, until I actually bought some, for the first time in my life, in order to bake madeleines. Imagine my shock when I opened the bottle. It smells like old lady hair tonic. I tried adding it once to my madeleine batter, instead of vanilla or citrus zest. It turned out, as the English would say worriedly, "a bit of a nightmare".

Most recipes say to add 1-2 tablespoons to the batter, which seems to me too much. The hair tonic smell remains strong even after baking. I had crafted not madeleines, but 16 crumbly soaps from a Victorian drugstore. They even tasted like soap.

I even made sure to buy the right kind of orange blossom water. It should be distilled from bitter orange flowers, and not just water with orange oil in it. Cortas is the brand everyone swears by. French versions exist: they are more expensive and I doubt that they're really made in France. (In Spain, I heard from a farming family that Valencia oranges sold as "from Valencia" were really grown in Tunisia, then shipped to be packaged in Valencia.) So between "French" and Middle-Eastern orange flower water, I decided on the latter. However, as I never got used to the smell, I now omit orange flower water entirely.

The problem with using lemon or citrus zest is that it just makes your madeleines lemony or orangey. So omit the citrus zest or the flavoring element if you don't care for it. I've seen people add pistachio, almond, Armagnac, and so on. Try if you like. I am suspicious of flavored madeleine recipes, the same way a real Italian grandma would never use flavored dry pasta or drink flavored coffee. I prefer neutral, buttery madeleines, but that's just me.

Many recipes call for cake flour. This threw me for a loop. What the hell is CAKE FLOUR? I had to find a definition on the Web. Some kinds of cake flour are nothing but ordinary all-purpose flour cut with cornstarch. That sounds disgusting. I read the label and bought cake flour that is 100% flour ("premium").

I've made madeleines with different kinds of flour. Madeleines came out more substantial and chewy when made with all-purpose flour (tastes like a cross between a cake and a cookie). Cake flour makes the madeleine too soft, like a sponge cake. I've tried mixing in a little whole wheat flour in once. Why, I don't know. It never tastes good. It just makes you feel virtuous because you're eating half a cup of butter in this project.

The best tasting madeleines I made, that had a really good shape and texture, were from Jovial 100% Organic Einkorn All-Purpose Flour. Einkorn is some kind of 'ancient', 'wild' wheat. Actually, it looks and smells just like ordinary white all-purpose flour, so maybe they're having us on, but it's such a crazy specialized item that I had to try it. I did like the result. Sure, it's more expensive than ordinary supermarket flour. But come on, how expensive can flour be? How much did you pay for that goddamned madeleine pan again? Go ahead. Treat yourself to specialty flour.

By the way, you notice that I said to use a hand-held mixer. If you have one of those giant, beautiful Kitchen-Aid stand mixers, you can use that, if you can find the original manual. Don't lose your fingers when you turn it on!

In *Mastering the Art of French Cooking*, I recall them saying something about using hand mixers because it's easier to move about and you can tilt the batter from the side to side to incorporate more air. I bet those old gals wrote pages and pages about hand mixers in that insane treatise, but I can't go check for you because I have the first edition and it's so dusty and falling apart that I will sneeze if I open it. The only piece of wisdom I can impart to you is this. If you're being cheap like me, and went to Target to buy a hand mixer because you stupidly forgot to register for one when you first got married, you may be forced to choose between 5 speeds, 6 speeds, 7 speeds, or 10 speeds.

What the hell?

What's the difference? Why on earth would I need more than five differentiated levels for beating eggs? Who cares? Besides, the 5-speed one came in cute, pastelly colors. The 10-speed one was brute black and looked like a spare part from a motorbike. I plonked for the cheap little 5 speed.

I regret. I realized, after actually using it to make madeleines, that higher speeds means *faster* whipping. So the more expensive the hand mixer, the more power it has, and the faster you will get your eggs to whisk, and your egg whites to 'mount', and so on. Damn.

Just as you should never save on powerful hairdryers, you should now learn not to save on powerful hand mixers. Unless you want to stand all day at the kitchen counter, with your hand crooked at an unnatural angle, mixing slowly.

By the way, a madeleine recipe I tried told me to beat the batter using the hand mixer for 10 minutes. This sounds reasonable until you actually do it. I don't believe the author actually ever used this recipe. It's not humanly possible to stand still and beat batter with a hand mixer for 10 whole minutes. Try it. You would be screaming with boredom after 120 seconds. Another example of cookbook authors' contempt for human rights.

My ideal kind of bump: nothing more, nothing less.

Actually, I do not know why the bump is such a big deal.

Step 3: Filling the Mold, More Chill Time (1 hour 10 minutes)

Clear a space in your fridge to hold the madeleine tray at the end of Step 3.

Filling the mold (the madeleine tray) is a critical step. However, all the recipes I've ever read never say anything more than "Butter the mold. Fill with batter." Come on. This is rocket science. I'm going to write pages about this step so you won't ever go wrong.

Butter the madeleine mold, then flour it by sifting flour over the buttered surface. Knock excess flour out over sink. No matter how nonstick your mold claims, try to do both — buttering and flouring — because it's not worth the risk of the thing sticking at the end of all this effort.

Savages use PAM spray. Never tried it, because I don't like to eat madeleines coated with PAM spray. However, I'm positive it's much more fool-proof than my method.

If you have a really fussy and pricey madeleine tray, the grooves will be very deep. This is because 'they' thought it would make for a fancier silhouette. 'They' just created more work for you.

Make sure the butter and flour go deep into the reaches of each of the grooves of the shell shape, because if the madeleine sticks in the grooves, when you pop them out, the ridges on the madeleine would not look as crisp as a properly-ironed pleat. They would appear marred – one or more of the ridges would look broken or blurred. Then you have to spend time cleaning the stuck bits out of each of the grooves by hand, which is really annoying.

The shell shape is actually a devilish detail and accomplishes very little except assure the world that French bakers are cleverer: anybody can make muffins from muffin trays but not everyone can easily pull off madeleines from madeleine trays.

Whenever I make 16 madeleines, no matter how careful I have been in buttering and flouring each groove, a full 4-6 of them would not be perfect because of the marred ridge issue. So, if you want 100% picture perfection, you'd better

Madeleines with marred ridges or blotchy surfaces from imperfect buttering and flouring of mold. They are also different colors because I failed to turn on the convection fan in the oven and heat was not distributed evenly.

Madeleines with perfect finish and crisp edges from properly buttered and floured mold. Most of the joy of madeleines is their cute final appearance, so I try to make them as picture-perfect as possible. Otherwise you might as well make muffins.

You do not want to see bits of batter stuck on the mold. This means the madeleine that popped out has a marred finish. Plus you now have to clean out the stuck bits. This is bullshit.

take this step seriously (unlike me). Do not worry about the flour sitting on the outside of the mold (the flat empty space between the molds on the tray). It wouldn't come to harm in the oven, and if your mold is nonstick, any flour on that flat part would be easy to clean off when you're washing up.Using two butter knives, spoon the cold batter into madeleine mold.

As the yoga teacher likes to say, remember to breathe.

The cold batter would be stiff enough for you to do this easily. Some people say "pipe the batter" into the mold, but why, you'll have a piping bag to clean up later (assuming you have one).

Fill each mold no more than 2/3 full as batter will expand when baking. You should have enough batter for 16 molds. But as you are filling, keep an eye on whether you're running out of batter and decide whether you want 12 big madeleines or 16 medium ones. If you cannot simultaneously make important decisions like that while spooning cookie batter, you should not operate a moving vehicle.

Overfilled molds runneth over; be prepared to live with the results of your own indiscretion.

If you lack the discipline to put the exact same amount of batter in each mold, just know that you'll end up baking madeleines of different sizes, heights, and even shapes (as overfilled molds will runneth over), so just be prepared to live with the results of your own indiscretion.

I'm sick of eating all the imperfect madeleines and saving the perfect ones for people I want to impress. So now I aim to make all 16 perfect out of my 16-mold tray, because *I* want to eat perfect madeleines too. But that's just me.

Put the filled tray back in fridge for 1 more hour. There is no need to plastic wrap it if you're just chilling for 1 more hour; but wrap it if you think you'll walk away and forget.

In the last 10-15 minutes of this hour while the batter is chilling, you can start pre-heating the oven.

Bon,
Almost There

Step 4: Baking In The Oven
(15 minutes max)

Make sure your oven rack is in the middle spot. Put a baking sheet in it. Preheat oven 425 F with the baking sheet in it. When I say 'preheat', make sure you let it preheat for minimum 10 minutes (if your oven heats up quickly like mine) or 15 minutes. Some recipes even say you can go up to 450 F: try if you dare.

Take the chilled madeleine tray out of the fridge and put it in the oven on the heated baking sheet. Make sure the oven is definitely super hot before putting the chilled madeleine tray in. You want the "thermal shock" because this helps form the madeleine "bump".

Set timer for 10 minutes.

ああああああ！ゴキブリだ！
THERE IS A COCKROACH ON THE WINDOW! HOW DID IT GET IN THE HOUSE?

Oh, it's on the outside. Phew. Gone.

Total time for baking is 11-13 minutes max, but check frequently to see how it's developing. Madeleines are easy to burn. Just so you won't walk away and do something else – like writing this book – and forget about it entirely, just plant yourself in front of the oven door and watch it. Ten minutes isn't that long: just enough to listen to Kreisler's *Prelude and Allegero in the Style of Puganini* twice to get into the mood of eating difficult European cookies.

Sometimes if your oven is uneven, the madeleines will not rise uniformly. So take this opportunity to quickly adjust the tray. Do not open the door too much or you will lose heat: just stick a chopstick or thongs in and move the tray. Rotating the tray at least once will promote even rising. You can see the 'bump' forming.

I've baked many madeleines. For many a long afternoon I have sat by the oven, watching the formation of the bump. I don't understand why madeleines bump. I refuse to Google the answer. I had a few theories. Today, I've decided on one. Brace yourself. The madeleine bumps because there is a lot of baking powder in there. As the madeleine (all that cold butter) melts in the heat of the oven, it starts to cook and then rise. The edges rise and solidify first, because they're on the outside of the concave mold. The middle part remains liquid and cold. By the time the heat reaches the Madeleine Core and cooks it, the Core begins to rise, but it has nowhere to go because it's surrounded by a casing of already solid cake. So it goes up. That's what causes the bump!

You can be sure one of those male 'scientific' celebrity cookbook writers has already written extensively about this issue. But I refuse to Google this to obtain corroboration. This is my

They're easy to burn. The exterior-interior color differentiation is too great. I still eat them. Grudgingly.

theory and I'm sticking to it.

Once that bump begins to fissure (it will look like a volcano cone eruption), it's almost done. If your oven holds heat really well like mine, you can turn it off and leave it for the last 2-3 minutes of the 13 minutes. At this point, the smell of baked buttery cookies will fill the kitchen. The edges would be slightly bubbling and beginning to brown. Don't let it burn to black!

Take it out and check for doneness: the madeleine middle should be springy to the touch. It's done with it's springy and the edges are a bit brown and crispy.

I like mine with a little bump with a fissure in the bump, and the edges browned and crispy, but the inside fluffy, chewy and springy.

Remove from oven. Remember to carefully and slowly pry them out with the help of a small butter knife because you don't want the marred ridges problem (see above). Let them cool on a wire rack so that they firm up a little before you eat.

Remember to assemble photographic evidence of the nice ones before you eat them, because nobody will ever believe that you made them. If you are one of those people who post online the results of their cooking, just to brag, you can spend some time posting your pictures now on your social networking site(s). Just know that the moment it goes live, tons of people will remember that you are lame.

They say madeleines go with hot English tea but I prefer mine with milk or coffee. You know why people dipped theirs in tea originally? Because their madeleines were already hard and stale, that's why. A fresh one that you baked yourself doesn't need to be dipped in anything. There's just so much butter in them that your tea would be oily, and who wants oily tea.

If you are feeling guilty about eating so much butter, you could try substituting 50% of the white flour in this recipe for whole wheat flour, and 50% of the butter for olive oil. I tried it and the madeleines came out more or less the same shape, with the same mouth feel, but they taste much more boring, I'm warning you.

If you have leftovers, put the cookies in airtight container and in the fridge. No matter what people say, they will still taste good after a few days.

C'est fini! Thank God. Now, take off your apron, pat yourself on the back. Carefully wash and wipe clean that beautiful madeleine pan and put it in the pile to donate to Goodwill.

The End

The Role of Cake
In Wena Poon's Novels

NOBODY BELIEVES ME, but a few academics – bless them – have written papers about my fiction. These have stern titles like "Wena Poon and the Politics of Race", "Wena Poon and the Postcolonial Short Story"…things like that. But all this time, what I really want to read is a thesis with a title like "Wena Poon and the Role of Cake". Since nobody has written it yet, I will write a little of it myself to get you started.

"What are you doing?" my husband asks, looking over my shoulder.

I froze. Now, you must know that nothing irritates novelists more than someone reading over their shoulder as they write.

"I am writing a paper about the role of cake in my own books," I replied.

Silence. Then, in a slow, measured tone of utter incredulity, "Do you realize that this Madeleine book that you are making…do you realize that *someone might actually buy it and read it?*"

"What's wrong with that?"

"HOW COULD YOU BE SO VAIN?"

"T.S. Eliot annotated his own poems."

"T.S. Eliot was an anti-Semite."

"Well, *I'm* not," I said.

Silence. Then he left the room.

Continuons.

Cherry Cake

The martial arts swordfighting trilogy, *Hoshimaruhon,* feature a rather mythical dessert called, simply, cherry cake, which was a favorite of Emperor Taliesin. His cousin, the Regent Edward Lord Paisley, authored a sex treatise in which cherry cake was carefully deliberated. Lord Paisley's extract appears in *Voyage to the Dark Kirin*, and is reprinted below with the permission of the author (Lord Paisley) and publisher (me).

AN EXTRACT FROM *Jing Erotica Plain & Simple*
Scroll 17, Chapter 2
The Jing Woman, Broken Down & Analyzed

For thousands of years, scholars and poets have agreed that the exemplary Jing Woman should model herself after a peach. See Figure 29-1.

She should be soft, fleshy and pretty on the outside, but hard and unyielding on the inside. The Jing Woman, despite her submissive exterior, has always been prized for her outstanding capability to rationalize pain and suffering and make the most extraordinary sacrifices. In times of war, she is ready to put on her Sunday best, grab her children, and bravely leap off a cliff, her makeup intact, rather than be captured by the enemy.

Times have changed.

Among our modern Jing womenfolk, a new

aesthetic prevails. The most stellar examples of Jing women are inverted peaches. Nay, they are not peaches at all. They are hard on the outside and have a sweet, molten core, if you can get to it. As Cousin Taliesin says, they are like his favorite dessert, cherry cake.

Cherry cake?

Cousin Taliesin may not know anything about sex, but on matters of Imperial Confectionary, he is an absolute master, having been indulged since birth as Emperor. He explains by enclosing his description for the Perfect Jing Cherry Cake:

Layers, from outside in:

(1) Golden millefeuille

(2) Almond paste (just a tiny bit to hold   (1) together)

(3) Dark chocolate shell

(4) Yellow sponge cake

(5) Green tea mochi

(6) Stewed cherries (or whipped cream, or custard, but cherry's best because more vegetarian).

See Figure 29-2.

I never would have guessed. On the outside, Jing cherry cakes don't look like much. They're just these little round cakes that you can hold in your hand and eat on the go. You can't even fathom the complicated colors, textures and flavors inside. The best cherry cake in the Imperial Palace is composed of as many as 2,180 alternating layers, but on the outside it looks exactly the same as store-bought, 3-layer cherry cake. You just don't know until you bite into it. "It takes a true connoisseur to appreciate the right layering technique," says Cousin Taliesin.

No longer a peach, then, the modern Jing Woman is a complicated confection. In times of war, she has redefined feminine bravery as riding out on the battlefield to attack the enemy with horse and spear. This is infinitely more practical from a military strategist's point of view, and less of a waste of human resources. If Jing women could fight, we could double the size of our fighting force. In times of peace, her surprising sweetness 'just bowls you over', simply because you were used to her being so damned tough. This is a very interesting new development in Jing sexuality. I can see this model taking off.

Frankly, I don't care if Jing women are peaches or cherry cake. I'd happily eat both.

If you want to know if Taliesin's cherry cake really exists, I would say no, I made it up, but close equivalents of it can be found in Singapore, Hong Kong, and Tokyo cake shops.

Baumkuchen

On a more serious note, *Café Jause* is about a group of Japanese, Chinese, and Jewish expatriates in 1930s Shanghai right before the outbreak of the Second World War. They get together in a Viennese bakery café in Shanghai to bake a traditional German *baumkuchen*.

The *baumkuchen* or *baumu* バウム is a popular cake in Japan, its rotund O shape in perfect harmony with East Asian ideas of happiness, perfection, and luck. It is so so very, very *maru* 丸 (round)!

Aside from *baumkuchen*, *Café Jause's* customers discuss Demel, the legendary Viennese café and bakery and home of the Sacher Torte. They also talk about other whimsical Austro-Hungarian pastries like the *Indianerkrapfen, Rigo Jancsi* and *Spanische Windtorte*. Don't you just love the names? Here is Irene and Irma, Hungarian Jewish sisters who fled Nazi Germany and run the café in Shanghai. They are talking to Arthur Hayashi, the Japanese officer who can speak German and who often goes incognito to their joint:

Irene appeared with a stack of kitchen towels for him to dry himself. "Long day, Herr Doktor? Like something to eat?"

He studied Irma's chalked menu on the wall. Then he pulled out his cigarette case and extracted a smoke. "What in God's name is a *Spanische Windtorte*?"

"You like meringue?"

"Not particularly."

"It's a multi-storied meringue cake."

"Like the dress you guys put Sis in?"

Irene turned to look at Sis. "The cake's even harder to assemble."

"How so?"

"We bake the top and bottom like a lid and a bottom. Then we bake these meringue rings and stack them. We glue everything together with more meringue. Then we fill the hollow interior with whipped cream and fruit, put the lid on, and pipe even more meringue and cream on top. Then we stud it with sugar violets – "

"Stop, please, I'm getting a headache."

"You have to eat it right away otherwise it will all dissolve into a mess."

"So when did you make it?" muttered Arthur, his lips clenched on a cigarette. He struck a match.

"Yesterday," said Irene nonchalantly. "Irma said it's practically inedible by now, but I didn't want to waste it, eggs being so expensive. Somebody might order it. There are at least two slices left."

"I'll order a slice to punish myself."

"'Kay. Tell me what you think. It's traditional but

I've never made it before."

"I didn't say I was actually going to eat it."

Unlike the book which you are holding in your hands, *Café Jause* isn't really about cakes and baking, of course. The baumkuchen in the novel is really a metaphor about society, about identity, about the rings of history that builds up over time, just like the rings of the bark of a tree – the original inspiration for the *baum* (tree) *kuchen* (cake). It's about how I really wished, on the 70th anniversary of the Second World War, that all these wonderful characters from different countries – products of an older cosmopolitan order – could have fixed things in 1936 so that we did not have to kill millions of people to put society back together again. We forget, but the world was already very international in the 1900s. East and West mingled liberally, and there were many romantic, cross-cultural stories.

Arthur looked over the brief menu. "You should make a *baumkuchen*."

"How would we set it up?" said Irene. "Don't you need a special machine?"

"According to what I was told in Tokyo," said Arthur. "The 'king of the cakes' was originally made by Romans roasting batter on a stick over an open spit. They used a tree branch. They didn't have a machine.

Don't make up excuses." He turned and translated for old Mr He, shaping a cylinder with his hands and a turning motion.

"Like roasting a sucking pig?" asked old Mr He.

Arthur turned to the sisters, satisfied. "Even the Chinese get it."

"It'll take many hours to coat each layer," said Irene.

"The best *baumkuchen*," said Pinkel. "Has more than twenty-five layers of cake."

"Who said so?" grunted Irma.

"I read about it in a magazine," said Pinkel.

"He reads good magazines," said Arthur.

"We simply can't afford to make such a huge cake," said Irene. "It'll take more eggs than we can get in a day."

Arthur leaned forward, his dark eyes intense. "I can get you all the eggs you need."

The sisters looked at each other. "But we don't even have a proper recipe."

"Shanghai's full of Germans," said Arthur. "Ask somebody. Don't complain your business isn't good if you can't even deliver a genuine *baumkuchen*. Why, even the Japanese can make *baumkuchen*. There's *baumkuchen* in Kobe. There's *baumkuchen* in Okinawa."

Everyone protested.

"Call yourself a baker and you can't even pull off the King of the Cakes," said Arthur.

Irene said she did not believe there was any *baumkuchen* in Japan. Irma said, where on earth is Okinawa, is that a newly-created country?

Arthur stubbed out his cigarette. "Sure there is *baumkuchen* in Japan. A German baker brought it to the German port in northeast China. Then he emigrated to Japan and set up shop there. You guys just don't know your desserts."

Pinkel said, "I actually remember reading about this in a magazine."

"All you need is a roasting spit," said Arthur.

"I'll write Mom for the recipe," said Pinkel. "She once told me it was made with the fewest ingredients possible. It's a question of technique and patience."

"The ultimate skill test," said Arthur. "If Café Jause can pull it off, then I can say I really have experienced everything in Shanghai."

By the way, what Author said is true. In the early 20th century, a German baker, Karl Juchheim, went to China, then Japan, and brought with him the European café and the *baumkuchen*. To this very day, you can buy Juchheim brand *baumkuchen* in Singapore and Tokyo. When I saw Juchheim in a department store, I teared up at the memory of this history. Few people know the story behind Juchheim.

I tend to cry over cake.

I had to set *Café Jause* in Shanghai, a city which I've actually been a few times, rather than in Vienna, because I had never been to Austria. I found out that there were Viennese cafes in Shanghai right up to the WWII years because of the Jewish exodus from Europe at the time. Once I realized this odd fact, the story practically wrote itself.

A couple of years after I wrote *Café Jause,* I finally had the chance to travel to Vienna. It was a schlep, but I made it. Demel turned out to be exactly as I had imagined. This ornate, multi-storied historic bakery café is a stone's throw from the Opera, the Spanish Riding School, and Doblinger, the classical sheet music shop where you can buy piano scores that you will never attempt. Cake, horses, and piano: all my favorite things in one city block.

I ate at Demel's every day. On my last day, I asked if I could speak with the manager. He was very surprised that an English-speaking Chinese woman wanted to meet him; he probably thought I was trying to sell something. I said quickly, before he could misunderstand, that I was a novelist and I had written a book about a Demel baker who went to China to found a Viennese café. He had started as a baker there himself, he said.

"Ah, it's our cookies on the cover," he said,

peering through his glasses.

"Why, yes, I ordered your cookies sent by mail to me in Texas. I wrote this book because I was craving for Viennese pastries but I couldn't get away at the time." I beamed. "And now I am here."

Butter Cake

Some time later, I found myself eating a *sandguglhupf* from Demel's. I do not know how to pronounce it, but it's the Viennese bundt cake, just made with a taller pan. I read that Demel's is so confident in the quality of its natural ingredients that it does not add vanilla or citrus zest to this buttery, eggy pound cake. When I ate it, I instantly remembered where else I have had this sort of non-flavored, honest-to-goodness cake...

Singapore! My aunt's family ran a bakery and cake shop. I used to hang out there when I was in kindergarten. I had completely forgotten to make the connection, but of course! That's why I like cakes!

Aunty's bakery was the corporate sponsor of all the birthday cakes of the children in the family, including this spectacular creation for me when I was four years old:

Note the strategically-dispersed maraschino
cherries, the creative use of clear, golden-yellow
jam to fill up the triangle of the '4'. As for the
glory of getting those papery wafer roses – hell
hath no fury like a child who is denied them (by
other children).

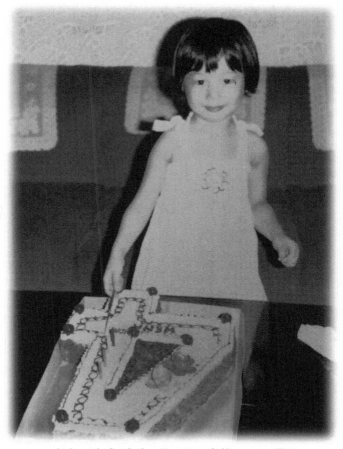

ありがとうございました, 家族のパン屋!

My aunt's family bakery was on the ground floor of an apartment block. It had its own immense ovens. Kids like me were never allowed to go to the mysterious back of the shop, because of all the scurrying bakers, huge mixers, and stacked stainless steel trays. It was always sweltering and smelled of superhot butter and oil. The only time I ever got to see any real kitchen action was at night, when the bakers took the bread rolls out to the open air front of the shop, laid them out on large tables, and sliced and filled them with ham, cheese, or cream. They would be chatting and slicing (with long, thin knives we were not allowed to touch) while I watched, fascinated. The men would be stripped to the waist, working in the heat of the tropical night, ignoring the cars and passersby.

"Give Wena a ham bun," my aunt would pipe up absently as she walked past. "Please someone give her a ham bun."

A fluffy, brioche-like round bun would appear before me, sliced almost two-thirds of the way and slathered with soft, real butter, with a pink tongue of a cooked ham slice inserted. Because I was family, sometimes I got *two* slices of ham, which made me feel really smug. As I ate, I watched customers buying ham buns. They had to pay, and they only got *one* slice of ham!

Some time later, my aunt would drift past again, on her way to another errand. "Give Wena a butter cake," she would murmur. "Wena, try the butter cake."

The butter cake, or as we say it in Singapore, *BA-tta kek,* is a slice of cake crafted to look exactly like the Portuguese *castella,* now ubiquitous in Japan. It measured about 2.5 by 3.25 inches — a crumbly, rich orange-yellow confection with a smooth, leathery-brown top. It was loaded with so much butter that a gentle prod would leave your fingertips slick with oil. For this reason, it always came demurely wrapped in its own wax paper doily.

A few moments later, my aunt, who remains, to this day, a very slender and beautiful lady, would come and find me, and ask anxiously, "Shall we go eat? Are you hungry?"

This was almost 35 years ago. Since then, Singapore has become a terribly expensive place. The cakes and breads of that bakery — European in origin, but styled in a particularly Southeast Asian way — are not replicable today. You would be hard-pressed to find a casual neighborhood place using fresh butter and making its own real cream.

I describe this bakery's confections in my very first book of short stories, *Lions In Winter.*

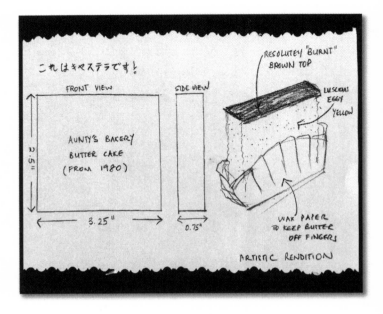

Strangely, of all the stories in that volume, the cake one is the one readers like to recount to me. It's the one they remember. Cakes, it turns out, are relatable. Literature, ordinarily, is not. I was at a small event at the Scottish Poetry Library in Edinburgh. I was asked to 'read something'. The audience had just sat through some lovely poetry presentations. It was my turn. It was just one of those grey days in Scotland. Hungry and cold, I decided to play the culture card. Instead of reading one of my poems, I read an extract from a Singapore story from *Lions In Winter*. It is called *Mrs Chan's Wedding Day*.

Still, I remember those hot afternoons, in Grandmother's dim kitchen, when Great Aunt so-and-so (also with a fresh perm for the occasion) brought over a box of assorted Western cakes, or a thick paper roll of Chinese biscuits that came apart in your hands; how they would gossip and laugh and congratulate each other, and talk about their children — every one of them in their turn, from oldest to youngest — while my younger cousin and I would peek into the cake box and secretly make up our minds which ones to eat once the guest had gone.

"I get the one with the cherry," I say when we retire to the bedroom, away from the grown-ups, to begin our usual consultation.

"Which one?" asks Winnie nervously, clasping her hands. "I saw two with cherries."

"The red cherry, not the green cherry."

"But you always get the red cherry!"

"Ok, ok!" I shout in alarm as she threatens to bawl. I make her a generous offer, "You can have the red cherry. I'll take the one with the chocolate rice all over on top. The all-chocolate jelly roll."

"But I want that one!"

"Why do you always want the one I want?" I shout. "I thought you want the red cherry one!"

Winnie is confused, and tries to cry again. I deliberate between locking her in the bedroom and going out to play by myself, or feigning indifference to every cake in the box, a ploy which usually works. I choose the latter, and we slide outside to be among the grown-ups again, each mentally running through the colorful possibilities in the big square cardboard box with the shiny thin grosgrain ribbon that is impossibly knotted at top speed by the lady behind the counter into a perfect bow. The square one in bright lizard green—the kaya cake—the bright yellow mango roll, the silent mauve one with blueberry on top, the virgin snow white rectangle with coconut. The pillowy egg roll with an irregular pattern burnt on its smooth outside that the Chinese bakers call "tiger skin." The dark, exotic smell of cocoa from the chocolate roll, and – the ones that kids don't like because there is no cream on them – the chiffony pandan cake and orange bundt cake.

These were the cakes of my aunt's family bakery. I had met them so many times growing up, they were like friends. They had, each and every one of them, a *distinct personality*.

I didn't think any Edinburgh resident would really know what I was talking about. But after the reading, a man came up to me and said, "I really enjoyed your piece. It was good to hear about cakes. *After all that poetry*."

Yes. Poetry is good for the soul. Cake is just good.

about the author

WENA POON's novels and short stories have been professionally produced on the London stage, serialized as a Book At Bedtime on BBC Radio 4, and extensively anthologized and translated into French, Italian, and Chinese. She won the UK's Willesden Herald Prize for best short fiction. She was also nominated for Ireland's Frank O'Connor Award, France's Prix Hemingway, the Singapore Literature Prize, and the UK's Bridport Prize for Poetry. Her fiction is studied by British, American, Hong Kong and Singapore academics as examples of transnational literature. From 2011 through 2017, her short stories are studied by thousands of Singapore high school students sitting for the Cambridge 'O' Level Exams in Literature. She graduated magna cum laude in English Literature from Harvard and holds a J.D. from Harvard Law School. She is a lawyer by profession. Her Web site is www.wenapoon.com.

有鑆氣

SUTAJIO WENA. BORN IN ASIA. MADE IN USA.

SUTAJIO WENA TITLES
スタジオウェナ の 本 カタログ

All books are in English.
Order from Amazon, Baker & Taylor, Ingram, and all major global distributors.

Cafe Jause

A Story of Viennese Shanghai

Wena Poon

Shanghai, 1936. All is not what it seems. On the eve of World War II, the Jewish, Chinese and Japanese customers of a famous Viennese café on Zhoushan Road get together for an international project: to bake the 'king of the cakes', the legendary German baumkuchen. ISBN-10: 1502549085. Available in paperback.

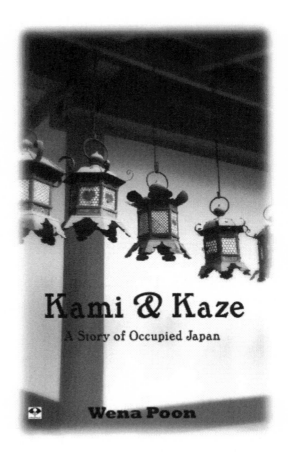

Kami & Kaze

A Story of Occupied Japan

Wena Poon

From 1945-1952, Japan was occupied by America. It was America's most significant experience of being a colonial government. For the Japanese, it was a period of suspicion and humiliation. For the Americans, it was a chance to experience a people they had only known across the battlefield. Despite the brevity of the contact, some Americans left with a lifelong love for the country. This is their story. ISBN-10: 1495921034. Available in paperback and Kindle.

THE ADVENTURES OF
SNOW FOX & SWORD GIRL

WENA POON

The young Emperor Taliesin has been wearing a silver mask ever since he was a child. No one has ever seen his face. Is he really the Son of Heaven? Or a fox spirit in human form? Annoyed by rumors, the Emperor sets off on a quest to prove that he is really human. Only his personal bodyguard, the divine swordswoman Sei Shonagon, knows the truth. *The Adventures of Snow Fox & Sword Girl* is a sophisticated fairy tale in Kurosawa costumes. A wonderfully funny, sexy, swashbuckling romp through the familiar landscape of Chinese and Japanese swordfighting epics, stylishly delivered, as its opening credits promise, "in modern English and in full Technicolor". ISBN-10: 1495957586. Available in paperback.

武
俠
小
說

VOYAGE TO THE DARK KIRIN

Wena Poon

Tired of administering his kingdom ever since he was a child, Taliesin, the Son of Heaven and the 33rd Emperor of Jing, decides to max out his budget. He sets sail with a hundred glorious treasure ships to hunt down the mythical black unicorn. "Shonagon's in charge," he announces to the appalled Ministers of Cabinet. Can the divine swordswoman Sei Shonagon outwit Machiavellian dukes, quell unruly ronin, and fight rebellious Noh ninja on her own? Or does she need help from the handsome but terribly prim priest, Takanoha? *Voyage to the Dark Kirin* is the second novel of the Hoshimaruhon series, a wonderfully funny, sexy, swashbuckling romp through the familiar landscape of Chinese and Japanese swordfighting epics, stylishly delivered, as its opening credits promise, "in modern English and in full Technicolor". Rated (R) for Adult Themes.

THE MARQUIS OF DISOBEDIENCE

WENA POON

A strange turn of Fate forces Emperor Taliesin to travel incognito in Jing as Scholar Ping: playwright and boy actress, famed for his sexual comedies for the Jing operatic stage. Convinced that she had lost him forever, Sei Shonagon disguises herself as a man and embarks on a mission for a haunted lute that would solve all her problems. Our story takes place nine years after *Voyage to the Dark Kirin* – enough time for the Barbarian Armies to multiply, Lord Paisley to finish building the Great Wall, and Takanoha's adopted daughters to grow up and start rattling their sabers. *The Marquis of Disobedience* is the third novel of the Hoshimaruhon series, a wonderfully funny, sexy, swashbuckling romp through the familiar landscape of Chinese literary classics and Japanese samurai epics, stylishly delivered, as its opening credits promise, "in modern English and in full Technicolor". Rated (R) for Adult Themes.

CHANG'AN

WENA POON

a Story of China & Japan

When Japan surrendered to the Allies at the end of WWII, approximately 6.5 million Japanese were left stranded outside of their country. In China alone there were 2.6 million Japanese, including many women and children, despised by the world and forgotten by their government. Determined to survive, the brilliant and mercurial military doctor Arthur Hayashi hid in Communist China for decades and left to his grand-daughter an unforgettable legacy. Named after the mythic Chinese city on which Kyoto was modeled, *Chang'an* is a refreshingly unconventional take on Japan, China and the modern quest to end decades of bitterness.

Recipe – Condensed Summary To Tear Out & Use

Step 1: Dry Ingredients Mixing (5 min)
Get ready 1 small mixing bowl and these things:
- 2/3 cup flour (all purpose)
- 1 teaspoon baking powder
- pinch of salt

Sift this stuff together into mixing bowl and then set it aside.

Step 2: Wet Ingredients Mixing, then Chill Time (1 hour 10 minutes)
Get ready your handheld electric whisk, and these things:
- ½ cup butter (unsalted)(if using salted butter, omit the pinch of salt in Step 1).
- 2 large eggs
- 1/3 cup sugar
- 2 tablespoons milk (bring to room temperature)
- 1 tablespoon honey
- Nice to have: Grated zest of 1 lemon (or orange)
- 1 teaspoon best quality vanilla extract

First, soften the butter in microwave.

Put sugar in bowl. Using pastry cutter or fingertips, rub sugar and zest together until they're moist and fragrant.

Add the 2 eggs. Using handheld electric whisk, whisk for 2 minutes until mixture thickens slightly.

Add the honey and vanilla. Whisk a bit more.

Gently, slowly fold in the flour in 3 separate batches with a spatula.

Now fold in the melted butter and stir gently.

Then stir in the room temperature milk.

The batter should now be smooth and shiny. Put plastic wrap on the top to keep it from drying out and put in fridge for 1 hour or up to 2 days.

Step 3: Filling the Mold, More Chill Time (1 hour 10 minutes)
Butter and flour the mold thoroughly. Using two butter knives, spoon the cold batter into madeleine mold. Fill each mold no more than 2/3 full as batter will expand when baking.

Chill for 1 hour.

In the last 10-15 minutes of this hour while the batter is chilling, you can start pre-heating the oven.

Step 4: Baking In The Oven (15 minutes max)
Make sure your oven rack is in the middle spot. Put a baking sheet in it. Preheat oven 425 F with the baking sheet in it. Then put madeleines in.

Total time for baking is 11-13 minutes max. Check after 10 minutes to see how it's developing. Adjust tray midway to promote even rising.

Once that bump begins to fissure it's almost done. If your oven holds heat really well like mine, you can turn it off and leave it for the last 2-3 minutes of the 13 minutes. At this point, the smell of baked buttery cookies will fill the kitchen. The edges would be slightly bubbling and beginning to brown.

Take it out and check for doneness.

"Who writes a book of only 66 pages?!"

– Husband

"Me. Baldesar Castiglione. Haven't you read *Etiquette For Renaissance Gentlemen?*"

– Publisher

Made in the USA
Middletown, DE
16 August 2021